a 13

Heart's Needle

THIS FIRST EDITION OF
HEART'S NEEDLE
IS LIMITED TO 1500 COPIES
PRINTED FROM TYPE BY
CLARKE & WAY AT
THE THISTLE PRESS
NEW YORK

W. D. Snodgrass

Heart's Needle

New York   Alfred A. Knopf

1959

ACKNOWLEDGMENTS: Thanks are due to the following periodicals, in which certain of the poems in this book first appeared, and who have kindly given permission for their inclusion here: *Botteghe Oscure, Epoch, The Fifties, Hudson Review, New World Writing, The New Yorker, The Paris Review, Partisan Review, Perspective,* and *The Western Review.* Similar thanks are due to Meridian Books for permission to include poems first published in *New Poets of England and America.* The poems entitled "Song" and "Papageno" (the latter originally entitled "The Magic Flute: to Janice") originally appeared in *The New Yorker.* W.D.S.

L. C. Catalog card number; 59–5430

© *William Snodgrass, 1959*

This is a BORZOI BOOK, *published by* ALFRED A. KNOPF, INC.

FIRST EDITION

Jan

Contents

Heart's Needle

Ten Days Leave

He steps down from the dark train, blinking; stares
At trees like miracles. He will play games
With boys or sit up all night touching chairs.
Talking with friends, he can recall their names.

Noon burns against his eyelids, but he lies
Hunched in his blankets; he is half awake
But still lacks nerve to open up his eyes;
Supposing it were just his old mistake?

But no; it seems just like it seemed. His folks
Pursue their lives like toy trains on a track.
He can foresee each of his father's jokes
Like words in some old movie that's come back.

He is like days when you've gone some place new
To deal with certain strangers, though you never
Escape the sense in everything you do,
"We've done this all once. Have I been here, ever?"

But no; he thinks it must recall some old film, lit
By lives you want to touch; as if he'd slept
And must have dreamed this setting, peopled it,
And wakened out of it. But someone's kept

His dream asleep here like a small homestead
Preserved long past its time in memory
Of some great man who lived here and is dead.
They have restored his landscape faithfully:

The hills, the little houses, the costumes:
How real it seems! But he comes, wide awake,
A tourist whispering through the priceless rooms
Who must not touch things or his hand might break

Their sleep and black them out. He wonders when
He'll grow into his sleep so sound again.

Returned to Frisco, 1946

We shouldered like pigs along the rail to try
And catch that first gray outline of the shore
Of our first life. A plane hung in the sky
From which a girl's voice sang: ". . . you're home once
      more."

For that one moment, we were dulled and shaken
By fear. What could still catch us by surprise?
We had known all along we would be taken
By hawkers, known what authoritative lies

Would plan us as our old lives had been planned.
We had stood years and, then, scrambled like rabbits
Up hostile beaches; why should we fear this land
Intent on luxuries and its old habits?

A seagull shrieked for garbage. The Bay Bridge,
Busy with noontime traffic, rose ahead.
We would have liberty, the privilege
Of lingering over steak and white, soft bread

Served by women, free to get drunk or fight,
Free, if we chose, to blow in our back pay
On smart girls or trinkets, free to prowl all night
Down streets giddy with lights, to sleep all day,

Pay our own way and make our own selections;
Free to choose just what they meant we should;
To turn back finally to our old affections,
The ties that lasted and which must be good.

Off the port side, through haze, we could discern
Alcatraz, lavender with flowers. Barred,
The Golden Gate, fading away astern,
Stood like the closed gate of your own backyard.

For R. M. Powell

He fed them generously who were his flocks,
Picked, shatterbrained, for food. Passed as a goat
Among his sheep, I cast off. Though hurled rocks
And prayers deranged by torment tossed our boat,
I could not silence, somehow, this defiant
Mind. From my fist into the frothed wake ran
The white eye's gluten of the living giant
I had escaped, by trickery, as no man.

Unseen where all seem stone blind, pure disguise
Has brought me home alone to No Man's land
To look at nothing I dare recognize.
My dead blind guide, you lead me here to claim
Still waters that will never wash my hand,
To kneel by my old face and know my name.

At the Park Dance

As the melting park
darkens, the firefly winks
to signal loving strangers
from their pavilion
lined with Easter colored
lights, fading out together

until they merge with
weathered huge trees and join
the small frogs, those warm singers;
and they have achieved
love's vanishing point
where all perspectives mingle,

where even the most
close things are indistinct
or lost, where bright worlds shrink,
they will grope to find
blind eyes make all one world;
their unseen arms, horizons.

Beyond, jagged stars
are glinting like jacks hurled
farther than eyes can gather;
on the dancefloor, girls
turn, vague as milkweed floats
bobbing from childish fingers.

Orpheus

Stone lips to the unspoken cave;
Fingering the nervous strings, alone,
I crossed that gray sill, raised my head
To lift my song into the grave
Meanders of unfolding stone,
Following where the echo led
Down blind alleys of our dead.

Down the forbidden, backward street
To the lower town, condemned, asleep
In blank remembering mazes where
Smoke rose, the ashes hid my feet
And slow walls crumpled, settling deep
In rubble of the central square.
All ruin I could sound was there.

At the charred rail and windowsill,
Widows hunched in fusty shawls,
This only once the Furies wept;
The watchdog turned to hear me till
Head by head forgot its howls,
Loosed the torn images it kept,
Let sag its sore jaws and slept.

Then to my singing's radius
Seethed faces like a pauper's crowd
Or flies of an old injury.
The piteous dead who lived on us
Whined in my air, anarchic, loud
Till my soft voice that set them free,
Lost in this grievous enemy,

Rose up and laid them in low slumbers;
I meant to see in them what dark
Powers be, what eminent plotters.
Midmost those hushed, downcast numbers
Starved Tantalus stood upright, stark,
Waistdeep where the declining waters
Swelled their tides, where Danaus' daughters

Dropped in full surf their unfilled tub;
Now leaned against his rolling stone
Slept Sisyphus beneath the hill;
That screaming half-beast, strapped at the hub,
Whom Juno's animal mist had known,
Ixion's wheel creaked and was still.
I held all hell to hear my will.

"Powers of the Underworld, who rule
All higher powers by graft or debt,
Within whose mortgage all men live:
No spy, no shining power's fool,
I think in the unthought worlds to get
The light you only freely give
Who are all bright worlds' negative

You gave wink in an undue crime
To love—strong even here, they say.
I sing, as the blind beggars sing,
To ask of you this little time
—All lives foreclose in their due day—
That flowered bride cut down in Spring,
Struck by the snake, your underling."

In one long avenue she was
Wandering toward me, vague, uncertain,
Limping a little still, the hair
And garments tenuous as gauze
And drifting loose like a white curtain
Vacillating in black night air
That holds white lilacs, God knows where.

"Close your eyes," said the inner ear;
"As night lookouts learn not to see
Ahead but only off one side,
As the eye's sight is never clear
But blind, dead center, you must be
Content; look not upon your bride
Till day's light lifts her eyelids wide."

I turned my back to her, set out
My own way back and let her follow
Like some curious albino beast
That prowls in areas of drought,
Lured past the town's slack doors, the hollow
Walls, the stream-bed lost in mist,
That breathless long climb, with no least

Doubt she must track me close behind;
As the actual scent of flesh, she must
Trail my voice unquestioning where.
Yet where the dawn first edged my mind
In one white flashing of mistrust
I turned and she, she was not there.
My hands closed on the high, thin air.

It was the nature of the thing:
No moon outlives its leaving night,
No sun its day. And I went on
Rich in the loss of all I sing
To the threshold of waking light,
To larksong and the live, gray dawn.
So night by night, my life has gone.

Papageno

For Janice

Far in the woods my stealthy flute
Had jailed all gaudy feathered birds
And brought their songs back true to life;
Equipped with lime and quick salt, fruit
And fifty linking nets of works
I went to whistle up a wife.

My mouth was padlocked for a liar.
Losing what old hands never seek
To snare in their most cunning art,
I starved till my rib cage was wire
Under a towel. I could not speak
To hush this chattering, blue heart.

I beat about dead bushes where
No song starts and my cages stand
Bare in the crafty breath of you.
Night's lady, spreading your dark hair,
Come take this rare bird into hand;
In that deft cage, he might sing true.

The Marsh

Swampstrife and spatterdock
  lull in the heavy waters;
some thirty little frogs
  spring with each step you walk;
a fish's belly glitters
  tangled near rotting logs.

Over by the gray rocks
  muskrats dip and circle.
Out of his rim of ooze
  a silt-black pond snail walks
inverted on the surface
  toward what food he may choose.

You look up; while you walk
  the sun bobs and is snarled
in the enclosing weir
  of trees, in their dead stalks.
Stick in the mud, old heart,
  what are you doing here?

September in the Park

This pinched face of the moon
   all afternoon
spies through the hanging smoke
that glows where maples, turning,
   recall for one
more hour the tarnished sun
in rust of their last burning.

Still, those who are out walking
   will hear the laughter
of drab, blue-chevroned ducks;
the drunkard echo mocking
   where they carouse
on minnow ponds still flowing.
Beyond the bare oak's
   reach of boughs,
as black as some charred rafter,
are slow and waiting flocks,
   but they are going.

This world is going
to leave the furnitures
of its unsheltering house
   in snow's dustcovers.
This old moon on its rounds
of the estate and grounds
   can well make sure
that no trespasser stirs
the fireplace or uncovers
   the burned out bed
of ashes. The young lovers

will not be coming here
    to give the bear
the offer of their bread.
This watchful face of age
    set pale and stern
over the gray iron cage
where his old habits turn
    and pace again
must mind his days to turn
him back in single, deep,
    cold-blooded sleep.

The hurrying, gray squirrels
    gather together
their hoard of the rich acorns
to their tall, windblown nest.
    And I, dear girl,
remember I have gathered
my hand upon your breast.

The Operation

From stainless steel basins of water
They brought warm cloths and they washed me,
From spun aluminum bowls, cold Zephiran sponges,
      fuming;
Gripped in the dead yellow glove, a bright straight razor
Inched on my stomach, down my groin,
Paring the brown hair off. They left me
White as a child, not frightened. I was not
Ashamed. They clothed me, then,
In the thin, loose, light, white garments,
The delicate sandals of poor Pierrot,
A schoolgirl first offering her sacrament.

I was drifting, inexorably, on toward sleep.
In skullcaps, masked, in blue-green gowns, attendants
Towed my cart, afloat in its white cloths,
The body with its tributary poisons borne
Down corridors of the diseased, thronging:
The scrofulous faces, contagious grim boys,
The huddled families, weeping, a staring woman
Arched to her gnarled stick,—a child was somewhere
Screaming, screaming—then, blind silence, the elevator
      rising
To the arena, humming, vast with lights; blank hero,
Shackled and spellbound, to enact my deed.

Into flowers, into women, I have awakened.
Too weak to think of strength, I have thought all day,
Or dozed among standing friends. I lie in night, now,
A small mound under linen like the drifted snow.
Only by nurses visited, in radiance, saying, Rest.
Opposite, ranked office windows glare; headlamps, below,
Trace out our highways; their cargoes under dark
        tarpaulins,
Trucks climb, thundering, and sirens may
Wail for the fugitive. It is very still. In my brandy bowl
Of sweet peas at the window, the crystal world
Is inverted, slow and gay.

So small it is, there must be at least two
Helping each other see it. If each stands
Close enough he may come to be foureyed
And make their sight bifocal, looking through
Each other. If they act as a microscope
Of mounted powers it shall be magnified
Like an airy globe or beach ball that expands
Between them so vast they could never hope
To grasp it without all four of their hands
                Opened wide.

It lengthens, outstretched like a playing field
Where they stand as the two opposing goals
That can't be reached. Or it's a field of force,
Ethereal continuum, whereby they wield
Influence through matter, time and space
(Of all which it's the grave and radiant source),
Yet where attraction drives out their like souls
Across the expansive universe they've built as the poles
That only in circumference embrace
                And by divorce.

You have the damnedest friends and seem to think
You have some right to think. You have kept keen
Our arguments and souls so we have grown
Closely together where most people shrink.
You sleep tonight with threatening relations
In El Dorado; I am here alone
To tell you, "*Vive la difference!*" We have seen
The energetic first stuff of creation
So that today, if there's a world between
        Us, it's our own.

Winter Bouquet

Her hands established, last time she left my room,
this dark arrangement for a winter bouquet:
collected bittersweet, brittle stemmed Scotch broom,
perennial straw-flowers, grasses gone to seed,
lastly, the dry vaginal pods of mildweed.
These relics stay here for her when she's away.

Bulging like a coin purse fallen on the ground
of damp woods, overgrained with moss, mould and frost,
their husks are horned like the Venus'-combs I found
on Garipan. Those war years, many a wife
wandered the fields after such pods to fill life
preservers so another man might not be lost.

Now she's home. Today I lifted them, like charms
in the March sunshine to part the pods and blow
white bursts of quilly weedseed for the wide arms
and eyes of the children squealing where they drift
across the neighbors' cropped lawns like an airlift
of satyrs or a conservative, warm snow.

Song

Observe the cautious toadstools
   still on the lawn today
though they grow over-evening;
   sun shrinks them away.
Pale and proper and rootless,
   they righteously extort
their living from the living.
   I have been their sort.

See by our blocked foundation
   the cold, archaic clay,
stiff and clinging and sterile
   as children mold at play
or as the Lord God fashioned
   before He breathed it breath.
The earth we dig and carry
   for flowers, is strong in death.

Woman, we are the rich
   soil, friable and humble,
where all our murders rot,
   where our old deaths crumble
and fortify my reach
   far from you, wide and free,
though I have set my root
   in you and am your tree.

Song

Sweet beast, I have gone prowling,
   a proud rejected man
who lived along the edges
   catch as catch can;
in darkness and in hedges
   I sang my sour tone
and all my love was howling
   conspicuously alone.

I curled and slept all day
   or nursed my bloodless wounds
until the squares were silent
   where I could make my tunes
singular and violent.
   Then, sure as hearers came
I crept and flinched away.
   And, girl, you've done the same.

A stray from my own type,
   led along by blindness,
my love was near to spoiled
   and curdled all my kindness.
I find no kin, no child;
   only the weasel's ilk.
Sweet beast, cat of my own stripe,
   come and take my milk.

Seeing You Have . . .

Seeing you have a woman
Whose loves grow thick as the weeds
That keep songsparrows through the year,
Why are you envious of boys
Who prowl the streets all night in packs
So they are equal to the proud
Slender girls they fear?

She's like the tall grass, common,
That sends roots, where it needs,
Six feet into the prairies.
Why do you teach yourself the loud
Hankering voices of blue jays
That quarrel branch by branch to peck
And spoil the bitter cherries?

Home Town

I go out like a ghost,
nights, to walk the streets
I walked fifteen years younger—
seeking my old defeats,
devoured by the old hunger,
I had supposed

this longing and upheaval
had left me with my youth.
Fifteen years gone; once more,
the old lies are the truth:
I must prove I dare,
and the world, and love, is evil.

I have had loves, had such
honors as freely came;
it does not seem to matter.
Boys swagger just the same
along the curbs, or mutter
among themselves and watch.

They're out for the same prize.
And, as the evening grows,
the young girls take the street,
hard, in harlequin clothes,
with black shells on their feet
and challenge in their eyes.

Like a young bitch in her season
she walked the carnival
tonight, trailed by boys;
then, stopped at a penny stall
for me; by glittering toys
the pitchman called the reason

to come and take a chance,
try my hand, my skill.
I could not look; bereft
of breath, against my will,
I walked ahead and left
her there without one glance.

Pale soul, consumed by fear
of the living world you haunt,
have you learned what habits lead you
to hunt what you don't want;
learned who does not need you;
learned you are no one here?

A Cardinal

I wake late and leave
the refurbished quonset
where they let me live.
I feel like their leftovers:
they keep me for the onset
of some new war or other.

With half a ream of paper
and fountain pens, equipped
with ink and ink eraser,
a book to hunt up words,
and the same old manuscripts,
I tromp off to the woods,

the little stand of birches
between golf course and campus
where birds flirt through the branches
and the city will be hushed.
Inside this narrow compass
I crash through underbrush,

beer cans and lovers' trash
in search of my horizons
of meadowlark and thrush.
Yet near me, here, it's still.
I carry a scared silence
with me like my smell.

At each of my footsteps
one of the insect noises
in the tall grass, stops.
The weeds sing where I leave.
All the living voices
evade me like beliefs.

Well, let them look *me* up
and take their own sweet time;
I've come to set up shop
under this blue spruce
and tinker at my rhymes.
God knows it's little use;

God knows I have spent ages
peering like a stuffed owl
at these same blank pages
and, though I strained to listen,
the world lay wrapped with wool
far as the ends of distance.

And what do I hear today?
Little that sounds mine—
in town, across the way,
mill whistles squeal;
now, closer by, the whine
of a freight car's wheels;

out on the superturnpike
the cattle trucks and trailers
lumbering toward next week;
beyond, from the county airport,
where golf balls veer like tracers,
great engines thunder their part

in this devil's Mass
of marketable praise.
Oh, they've all found *their* voices.
And now I catch a meter
under this heavy prose
of factories and motors:

the college air cadets
are on their grinder, marching,
counting out their cadence,
one two three four, creating
for the school and market
the ground bass of our credo—

faith in free enterprise
and our unselfish forces
who chant to advertise
the ancient pulse of violence.
Meantime, I fuss with phrases
or clamp my jaws in silence.

Watch out; what's this red
bird, fluttering up to perch
ten feet from my head!
See the green insect wings,
pinched in his beak, twitch.
He swallows it. And sings.

Speak of the bloody devil!
Old sleek satanic cardinal—
you get your bellyful,
maintain the ancient Law,
and celebrate this ordinal
of the red beak and claw.

You natural Jesuit,
sing, in your fine feathers,
Hosannah to Appetite;
announce to the woods and hills
the one god of our fathers
is living in us still;

sing for the flyboys, birdy,
in praise of their profession;
sing for the choirs of pretty
slogans and catch-phrases
that rule us by obsession;
praise what it pays to praise:

praise soap and garbage cans,
join with the majority
in praising man-eat-man,
or praise the young who sell
their minds to retire at forty.
With honor.
                    Go to hell!

Good God! This is absurd!
A veritable scarecrow!
I curse out a poor bird
for daring feed his belly;
now my bird has flown
and left me in this gully.

It is absurd, absurd
Darwinian self-pity!
As if a self-made bird
would sign his days to sergeants,
his soul to a committee,
or call himself a bargain!

As if I'd never heard
what the birds' song means;
as if I'd ask a bird
to mortify his body.
Wait; from the next ravine,
he's singing again, already.

And he outspeaks a vital
claim to know his needs;
his song's a squatter's title
on his tree and the half acre
in which he hunts and breeds
and feeds the best he's able.

To enemies and rivals,
to mates and quick beetles,
he sings out for survival:
"I want my meals and loving;
I fight nobody's battles;
don't pardon me for living.

The world's not done to me;
it is what I do;
whom I speak shall be;
I music out my name
and what I tell is who
in all the world I am."

We whistle in the dark
of a region in doubt
where unknown powers work,
as watchmen in the night
ring bells to say, *Watch out,
I am here; I have the right.*

It should be recognized
I have not come sneaking
and look for no surprises.
Lives are saved this way.
Each trade has its way of speaking,
each bird its name to say.

We whistle in the dark
to drive the devils off.
Each dog creates his bark.
Even I, in Navy blues,
I whistled *Wachet Auf*
to tell the sailors who.

He's back; obliquely flying
under a trail of vapor,
our sky's white center-line.
A robin goes by, wrestling
a streamer of toiletpaper
his mate might want for nesting.

Selfish, unorthodox,
they live upon our leavings.
Boys or cats or hawks
can scare them out of song.
Still, long as they are living,
they are not still for long.

Each year the city leaves
less of trees or meadows;
they nest in our very eaves
and say what they have to say.
Assertion is their credo;
style tells their policy.

All bugs, now, and the birds
witness once more their voices
though I'm still in their weeds
tracking my specimen words,
replenishing the verses
of nobody else's world.

The Campus on the Hill

Up the reputable walks of old established trees
They stalk, children of the *nouveaux riches*; chimes
Of the tall Clock Tower drench their heads in blessing:
"I don't wanna play at your house;
I don't like you any more."
My house stands opposite, on the other hill,
Among meadows, with the orchard fences down and
        falling;
Deer come almost to the door.
You cannot see it, even in this clearest morning.
White birds hang in the air between
Over the garbage landfill and those homes thereto
        adjacent,
Hovering slowly, turning, settling down
Like the flakes sifting imperceptibly onto the little town
In a waterball of glass.
And yet, this morning, beyond this quiet scene,
The floating birds, the backyards of the poor,
Beyond the shopping plaza, the dead canal, the hillside
        lying tilted in the air,
Tomorrow has broken out today:
Riot in Algeria, in Cyprus, in Alabama;
Aged in wrong, the empires are declining,
And China gathers, soundlessly, like evidence.
What shall I say to the young on such a morning?—
Mind is the one salvation?—also grammar?—
No; my little ones lean not toward revolt. They
Are the Whites, the vaguely furiously driven, who resist
Their souls with such passivity
As would make Quakers swear. All day, dear Lord, all day
They wear their godhead lightly.

They look out from their hill and say,
To themselves, "We have nowhere to go but down;
The great destination is to stay."
Surely the nations will be reasonable;
They look at the world—don't they?—the world's way?
The clock just now has nothing more to say.

These Trees Stand . . .

These trees stand very tall under the heavens.
While *they* stand, if I walk, all stars traverse
This steep celestial gulf their branches chart.
Though lovers stand at sixes and at sevens
While civilizations come down with the curse,
Snodgrass is walking through the universe.

I can't make any world go around *your* house.
But note this moon. Recall how the night nurse
Goes ward-rounds, by the mild, reflective art
Of focusing her flashlight on her blouse.
Your name's safe conduct into love or verse;
Snodgrass is walking through the universe.

Your name's absurd, miraculous as sperm
And as decisive. If you can't coerce
One thing outside yourself, why you're the poet!
What irrefrangible atoms whirl, affirm
Their destiny and form Lucinda's skirts!
She can't make up your mind. Soon as you know it,
Your firmament grows touchable and firm.
If all this world runs battlefield or worse,
Come, let us wipe our glasses on our shirts:
Snodgrass is walking through the universe.

April Inventory

The green catalpa tree has turned
All white; the cherry blooms once more.
In one whole year I haven't learned
A blessed thing they pay you for.
The blossoms snow down in my hair;
The trees and I will soon be bare.

The trees have more than I to spare.
The sleek, expensive girls I teach,
Younger and pinker every year,
Bloom gradually out of reach.
The pear tree lets its petals drop
Like dandruff on a tabletop.

The girls have grown so young by now
I have to nudge myself to stare.
This year they smile and mind me how
My teeth are falling with my hair.
In thirty years I may not get
Younger, shrewder, or out of debt.

The tenth time, just a year ago,
I made myself a little list
Of all the things I'd ought to know,
Then told my parents, analyst,
And everyone who's trusted me
I'd be substantial, presently.

I haven't read one book about
A book or memorized one plot.
Or found a mind I did not doubt.
I learned one date. And then forgot.
And one by one the solid scholars
Get the degrees, the jobs, the dollars.

And smile above their starchy collars.
I taught my classes Whitehead's notions;
One lovely girl, a song of Mahler's.
Lacking a source-book or promotions,
I showed one child the colors of
A luna moth and how to love.

I taught myself to name my name,
To bark back, loosen love and crying;
To ease my woman so she came,
To ease an old man who was dying.
I have not learned how often I
Can win, can love, but choose to die.

I have not learned there is a lie
Love shall be blonder, slimmer, younger;
That my equivocating eye
Loves only by my body's hunger;
That I have forces, true to feel,
Or that the lovely world is real.

While scholars speak authority
And wear their ulcers on their sleeves,
My eyes in spectacles shall see
These trees procure and spend their leaves.
There is a value underneath
The gold and silver in my teeth.

Though trees turn bare and girls turn wives,
We shall afford our costly seasons;
There is a gentleness survives
That will outspeak and has its reasons.
There is a loveliness exists,
Preserves us, not for specialists.

Heart's Needle

For Cynthia

" 'Your father is dead.' 'That grieves me,' said he.
'Your mother is dead,' said the lad. 'Now all pity
for me is at an end,' said he. 'Your brother is dead,'
said Loingsechan. 'I am sorely wounded by that,'
said Suibne. 'Your daughter is dead,' said Loingsechan. 'And an only daughter is the needle of the
heart,' said Suibne. 'Dead is your son who used to
call you "Father," ' said Loingsechan. 'Indeed,'
said he, 'that is the drop that brings a man to the
ground.' "

FROM AN OLD IRISH STORY,
THE FRENZY OF SUIBNE,
AS TRANSLATED BY MYLES DILLON

I

Child of my winter, born
When the new fallen soldiers froze
In Asia's steep ravines and fouled the snows,
When I was torn

By love I could not still,
By fear that silenced my cramped mind
To that cold war where, lost, I could not find
My peace in my will,

All those days we could keep
Your mind a landscape of new snow
Where the chilled tenant-farmer finds, below,
His fields asleep

In their smooth covering, white
As quilts to warm the resting bed
Of birth or pain, spotless as paper spread
For me to write,

And thinks: Here lies my land
Unmarked by agony, the lean foot
Of the weasel tracking, the thick trapper's boot;
And I have planned

My chances to restrain
The torments of demented summer or
Increase the deepening harvest here before
It snows again.

2

Late April and you are three; today
   We dug your garden in the yard.
To curb the damage of your play,
  Strange dogs at night and the moles tunneling,
   Four slender sticks of lath stand guard
    Uplifting their thin string.

So you were the first to tramp it down.
    And after the earth was sifted close
You brought your watering can to drown
All earth *and* us. But these mixed seeds are pressed
   With light loam in their steadfast rows.
    Child, we've done our best.

Someone will have to weed and spread
    The young sprouts. Sprinkle them in the hour
When shadow falls across their bed.
You should try to look at them every day
   Because when they come to full flower
    I will be away.

3

The child between them on the street
Comes to a puddle, lifts his feet
   And hangs on their hands. They start
At the live weight and lurch together,
Recoil to swing him through the weather,
   Stiffen and pull apart.

We read of cold war soldiers that
Never gained ground, gave none, but sat
   Tight in their chill trenches.
Pain seeps up from some cavity
Through the ranked teeth in sympathy;
   The whole jaw grinds and clenches

Till something somewhere has to give.
It's better the poor soldiers live
   In someone else's hands
Than drop where helpless powers fall
On crops and barns, on towns where all
   Will burn. And no man stands.

For good, they sever and divide
Their won and lost land. On each side
    Prisoners are returned
Excepting a few unknown names.
The peasant plods back and reclaims
    His fields that strangers burned

And nobody seems very pleased.
It's best. Still, what must not be seized
    Clenches the empty fist.
I tugged your hand, once, when I hated
Things less: a mere game dislocated
    The radius of your wrist.

Love's wishbone, child, although I've gone
As men must and let you be drawn
    Off to appease another,
It may help that a Chinese play
Or Solomon himself might say
    I am your real mother.

4

No one can tell you why
the season will not wait;
the night I told you I
must leave, you wept a fearful rate
to stay up late.

Now that it's turning Fall,
we go to take our walk
among municipal
flowers, to steal one off its stalk,
to try and talk.

We huff like windy giants
scattering with our breath
gray-headed dandelions;
Spring is the cold wind's aftermath.
The poet saith.

But the asters, too, are gray,
ghost-gray. Last night's cold
is sending on their way
petunias and dwarf marigold.
hunched sick and old.

Like nerves caught in a graph,
the morning-glory vines
frost has erased by half
still scrawl across their rigid twines.
Like broken lines

of verses I can't make.
In its unraveling loom
we find a flower to take,
with some late buds that might still bloom,
back to your room.

Night comes and the stiff dew.
I'm told a friend's child cried
because a cricket, who
had minstreled every night outside
her window, died.

5

Winter again and it is snowing;
Although you are still three,
You are already growing
Strange to me.

You chatter about new playmates, sing
Strange songs; you do not know
Hey ding-a-ding-a-ding
Or where I go

Or when I sang for bedtime, *Fox*
Went out on a chilly night,
Before I went for walks
And did not write;

You never mind the squalls and storms
That are renewed long since;
Outside, the thick snow swarms
Into my prints

And swirls out by warehouses, sealed,
Dark cowbarns, huddled, still,
Beyond to the blank field,
The fox's hill

Where he backtracks and sees the paw,
Gnawed off, he cannot feel;
Conceded to the jaw
Of toothed, blue steel.

6

Easter has come around
again; the river is rising
    over the thawed ground
and the banksides. When you come you bring
    an egg dyed lavender.
We shout along our bank to hear
our voices returning from the hills to meet us.
    We need the landscape to repeat us.

You lived on this bank first.
While nine months filled your term, we knew
    how your lungs, immersed
in the womb, miraculously grew
    their useless folds till
the fierce, cold air rushed in to fill
them out like bushes thick with leaves. You took your hour,
    caught breath, and cried with your full lung power.

Over the stagnant bight
we see the hungry bank swallow
    flaunting his free flight
still; we sink in mud to follow
    the killdeer from the grass
that hides her nest. That March there was
rain; the rivers rose; you could hear killdeers flying
    all night over the mudflats crying.

You bring back how the red-
winged blackbird shrieked, slapping frail wings,
    diving at my head—
I saw where her tough nest, cradled, swings
    in tall reeds that must sway
with the winds blowing every way.
If you recall much, you recall this place. You still
    live nearby—on the opposite hill.

    After the sharp windstorm
of July Fourth, all that summer
    through the gentle, warm
afternoons, we heard great chain saws chirr
    like iron locusts. Crews
of roughneck boys swarmed to cut loose
branches wrenched in the shattering wind, to hack free
    all the torn limbs that could sap the tree.

    In the debris lay
starlings, dead. Near the park's birdrun
    we surprised one day
a proud, tan-spatted, buff-brown pigeon.
    In my hands she flapped so
fearfully that I let her go.
Her keeper came. And we helped snarl her in a net.
    You bring things I'd as soon forget.

You raise into my head
a Fall night that I came once more
   to sit on your bed;
sweat beads stood out on your arms and forehead and you wheezed for breath,
for help, like some child caught beneath
its comfortable woolly blankets, drowning there.
   Your lungs caught and would not take the air.

   Of all things, only we
have power to choose that we should die;
   nothing else is free
in this world to refuse it. Yet I,
   who say this, could not raise
myself from bed how many days
to the thieving world. Child, I have another wife,
   another child. We try to choose our life.

7

Here in the scuffled dust
   is our ground of play.
I lift you on your swing and must
   shove you away,
see you return again,
   drive you off again, then

stand quiet till you come.
   You, though you climb
higher, farther from me, longer,
   will fall back to me stronger.
Bad penny, pendulum,
   you keep my constant time

to bob in blue July
   where fat goldfinches fly
over the glittering, fecund
   reach of our growing lands.
Once more now, this second,
   I hold you in my hands.

8

I thumped on you the best I could
    which was no use;
you would not tolerate your food
until the sweet, fresh milk was soured
    with lemon juice.

That puffed you up like a fine yeast.
    The first June in your yard
like some squat Nero at a feast
you sat and chewed on white, sweet clover.
    That is over.

When you were old enough to walk
    we went to feed
the rabbits in the park milkweed;
saw the paired monkeys, under lock,
    consume each other's salt.

Going home we watched the slow
stars follow us down Heaven's vault.
You said, let's catch one that comes low,
    pull off its skin
    and cook it for our dinner.

    As absentee bread-winner,
I seldom got you such cuisine;
we ate in local restaurants
or bought what lunches we could pack
    in a brown sack

with stale, dry bread to toss for ducks
    on the green-scummed lagoons,
crackers for porcupine and fox,
life-savers for the footpad coons
        to scour and rinse,

snatch after in their muddy pail
    and stare into their paws.
When I moved next door to the jail
        I learned to fry
omelettes and griddlecakes so I

could set you supper at my table.
As I built back from helplessness,
        when I grew able,
the only possible answer was
    you had to come here less.

This Hallowe'en you come one week.
        You masquerade
    as a vermilion, sleek,
fat, crosseyed fox in the parade
or, where grim jackolanterns leer,

go with your bag from door to door
foraging for treats. How queer:
    when you take off your mask
my neighbors must forget and ask
        whose child you are.

Of course you lose your appetite,
    whine and won't touch your plate;
        as local law
I set your place on an orange crate
in your own room for days. At night

you lie asleep there on the bed
    and grate your jaw.
Assuredly your father's crimes
    are visited
on you. You visit me sometimes.

The time's up. Now our pumpkin sees
    me bringing your suitcase.
        He holds his grin;
the forehead shrivels, sinking in.
You break this year's first crust of snow

off the runningboard to eat.
    We manage, though for days
I crave sweets when you leave and know
they rot my teeth. Indeed our sweet
    foods leave us cavities.

9

I get numb and go in
though the dry ground will not hold
    the few dry swirls of snow
and it must not be very cold.
A friend asks how you've been
        and I don't know

or see much right to ask.
Or what use it could be to know.
    In three months since you came
the leaves have fallen and the snow;
your pictures pinned above my desk
        seem much the same.

Somehow I come to find
myself upstairs in the third floor
    museum's halls,
walking to kill my time once more
among the enduring and resigned
        stuffed animals,

where, through a century's
caprice, displacement and
    known treachery between
its wars, they hear some old command
and in their peacable kingdoms freeze
        to this still scene,

Nature Morte. Here
by the door, its guardian,
   the patchwork dodo stands
where you and your stepsister ran
laughing and pointing. Here, last year,
      you pulled my hands

   and had your first, worst quarrel,
so toys were put up on your shelves.
   Here in the first glass cage
the little bobcats arch themselves,
still practicing their snarl
      of constant rage.

   The bison, here, immense,
shoves at his calf, brow to brow,
   and looks it in the eye
to see what is it thinking now.
I forced you to obedience;
      I don't know why.

   Still the lean lioness
beyond them, on her jutting ledge
   of shale and desert shrub,
stands watching always at the edge,
stands hard and tanned and envious
      above her cub;

with horns locked in tall heather,
two great Olympian Elk stand bound,
    fixed in their lasting hate
till hunger brings them both to ground.
Whom equal weakness binds together
    none shall separate.

    Yet separate in the ocean
of broken ice, the white bear reels
    beyond the leathery groups
of scattered, drab Arctic seals
arrested here in violent motion
    like Napoleon's troops.

    Our states have stood so long
At war, shaken with hate and dread,
    they are paralyzed at bay;
once we were out of reach, we said,
we would grow reasonable and strong.
    Some other day.

    Like the cold men of Rome,
we have won costly fields to sow
    in salt, our only seed.
Nothing but injury will grow.
I write you only the bitter poems
    that you can't read.

Onan who would not breed
a child to take his brother's bread
    and be his brother's birth,
rose up and left his lawful bed,
went out and spilled his seed
        in the cold earth.

    I stand by the unborn,
by putty-colored children curled
    in jars of alcohol,
that waken to no other world,
unchanging where no eye shall mourn.
        I see the caul

    that wrapped a kitten, dead.
I see the branching, doubled throat
    of a two-headed foal;
I see the hydrocephalic goat;
here is the curled and swollen head,
        there, the burst skull;

    skin of a limbless calf;
a horse's foetus, mummified;
    mounted and joined forever,
the Siamese twin dogs that ride
belly to belly, half and half,
        that none shall sever.

I walk among the growths,
by gangrenous tissue, goitre, cysts,
    by fistulas and cancers,
where the malignancy man loathes
is held suspended and persists.
    And I don't know the answers.

    The window's turning white.
The world moves like a diseased heart
    packed with ice and snow.
Three months now we have been apart
less than a mile. I cannot fight
        or let you go.

10

The vicious winter finally yields
 the green winter wheat;
the farmer, tired in the tired fields
 he dare not leave will eat.

Once more the runs come fresh; prevailing
 piglets, stout as jugs,
harry their old sow to the railing
 to ease her swollen dugs

and game colts trail the herded mares
 that circle the pasture courses;
our seasons bring us back once more
 like merry-go-round horses.

With crocus mouths, perennial hungers,
 into the park Spring comes;
we roast hot dogs on old coat hangers
 and feed the swan bread crumbs,

pay our respects to the peacocks, rabbits,
 and leathery Canada goose
who took, last Fall, our tame white habits
 and now will not turn loose.

In full regalia, the pheasant cocks
    march past their dubious hens;
the porcupine and the lean, red fox
    trot around bachelor pens

and the miniature painted train
    wails on its oval track:
you said, I'm going to Pennsylvania!
    and waved. And you've come back.

If I loved you, they said, I'd leave
    and find my own affairs.
Well, once again this April, we've
    come around to the bears;

punished and cared for, behind bars,
    the coons on bread and water
stretch thin black fingers after ours.
    And you are still my daughter.

A Note on the Author

W(ILLIAM) D(E WITT) SNODGRASS was born in Wilkinsburg, Pennsylvania, on January 5, 1926. He attended Geneva College (Beaver Falls) and the State University of Iowa. He has taught at Cornell University and the University of Rochester, and also at the Morehead (Kentucky) and Antioch writers' conferences. Mr. Snodgrass, who is married and the father of three children, lives in Scottsville, New York. He was the 1958 Hudson Review Fellow in Poetry, and *Heart's Needle* won the first $1000 award in poetry of The Ingram Merrill Foundation.

A Note on the Production

THE TEXT *of this book was set on the Monotype in a typeface called* WALBAUM, *cut early in the nineteenth century by J. E. Walbaum, a type founder at Goslar and Weimar, who followed Didot in the design of this modern face. His original matrices are still in existence, and are the property of the Berthold Foundry, of Berlin, Germany.*

This first edition of HEART'S NEEDLE *consists of* 1500 *copies printed from type. The book was composed and printed by* CLARKE & WAY *at* THE THISTLE PRESS, *New York. The paper was manufactured by* S. D. WARREN COMPANY, *Boston. Bound by* H. WOLFF, *New York. Designed by* HARRY FORD.